What I Want

by Kathryn O'Dell

Illustrated by Eva Sassin

OXFORD
UNIVERSITY PRESS

OXFORD
UNIVERSITY PRESS

198 Madison Avenue
New York, NY 10016 USA

Great Clarendon Street, Oxford, OX2 6DP, United Kingdom

Oxford University Press is a department of the University of Oxford.
It furthers the University's objective of excellence in research, scholarship,
and education by publishing worldwide. Oxford is a registered trademark
|of Oxford University Press in the UK and in certain other countries

General Manager, American ELT: Laura Pearson
Executive Publishing Manager: Shelagh Speers
Senior Managing Editor: Anne Stribling
Senior Development Editor: Jennifer Wos
Development Editor: Diana Nott
Art, Design and Production Director: Susan Sanguily
Design Manager: Lisa Donovan
Designer: Jessica Balaschak
Electronic Production Manager: Julie Armstrong
Production Artist: Elissa Santos
Image Manager: Trisha Masterson
Image Manager: Joe Kassner
Production Coordinator: Christopher Espejo

ISBN: 978 0 19 458904 8

Printed in China

This book is printed on paper from certified and well-managed sources

Phonics words

apple   hat

banana   kite

doll   leaf

egg

Sight words

a   like

an   my

have   want

I

Activities

A Circle.

1.

c   f   a

2.

b   k   g

3.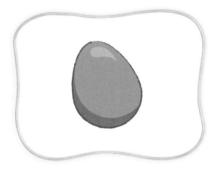

l   e   i

4.

d   j   h

B Circle.

1.

2. **d**

3. **l**

1.  • •

2.  • •

3. 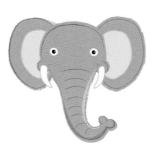 • •

4.  • •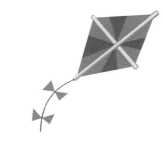

What do they want? Circle.

1.

2.

3.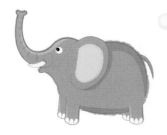

4.

Notes

Before reading

- Children point to the cover and name things they know.
- Children try to read the title.

While reading

- Children listen to the story. Point to the pictures as they listen. This will help them understand the story. Example: Point to the gorilla and the apple on page 4 for *I have an apple*.
- Children listen to the story again and read along.
- Children read the story. Help them with words they do not know.

After reading

- Children point to the pictures and name things they know.
- Children read the phonics words and sight words on page 3.
- Children take on the role of one of the characters. Role-play the story.
- Cover up some words in the story. Read the story and stop at each covered-up word. Children say the missing word.
- Children do all the activities on pages 12–15. Check answers with the children.
- Children talk about the story. What did they like?